ELMHURST PUBLIC LIBRARY

3 1135 01027 0577

W9-AXK-840

747.3
One

CountryLiving
150 Ways
to Dress Your
Windows

HEARST BOOKS
A division of Sterling Publishing Co., Inc.

New York / London
www.sterlingpublishing.com

ELMHURST PUBLIC LIBRARY
125 S. Prospect Avenue
Elmhurst, IL 60126-3298

Copyright © 2011 by Sterling Publishing Co., Inc.

All rights reserved. The written instructions and photographs in this volume are intended for the personal use of the reader and may be reproduced for that purpose only. Any other use, especially commercial use, is forbidden under law without the written permission of the copyright holder.

Every effort has been made to ensure that all the information in this book is accurate. However, due to differing conditions, tools, and individual skills, the publisher cannot be responsible for any injuries, losses, and/or other damages that may result from the use of the information in this book.

Design by woolypear

Library of Congress Cataloging-in-Publication Data
Spier, Carol.
150 Ways to Dress Your Windows / Carol Spier. — 1st ed.
p. cm.
Includes index.
ISBN 978-1-58816-546-6
1. Windows in interior decoration. I. Title.
NK2121.S65 2010
747'.3 — dc22
2009046022

10 9 8 7 6 5 4 3 2 1

Published by Hearst Books
A Division of Sterling Publishing Co., Inc.
387 Park Avenue South, New York, NY 10016

Country Living is a trademark of Hearst Communications, Inc.

www.countryliving.com

For information about custom editions, special sales, premium and corporate purchases,
please contact Sterling Special Sales Department at 800-805-5489 or specialsales@sterlingpub.com.

Distributed in Canada by Sterling Publishing
c/o Canadian Manda Group, 165 Dufferin Street
Toronto, Ontario, Canada M6K 3H6

Distributed in Australia by Capricorn Link (Australia) Pty., Ltd.
P.O. Box 704, Windsor, NSW 2756 Australia

Manufactured in China

Sterling ISBN 978-1-58816-546-6

Silk taffeta drapes hang gracefully in this room, with the sunlight accenting the beauty of their shimmering folds. Dressmaker details such as heavy pleating and smocking adorn the panels at the top, where they are attached to rings for easy opening and closing. The dark curtain rods call attention to the smocking and pick up the chocolate tones of the carpet, lamp, urn, and other furnishings.

Foreword

Just as a beautiful frame adorns a painting, a beautiful window treatment can be the perfect finishing touch for a room. And like a frame, the designs you choose to decorate your windows can be either understated or eye-catching. Whatever your personal taste, the attention you pay to this final decorating detail will be well worth the effort.

But where to begin? At *Country Living*, we believe a great place to start is to scour magazines and design books for inspiration. Well, look no further. On the pages ahead, you'll find more than 150 photographs depicting flowing drapes, wooden blinds, lace curtains, louvered shutters, roman shades, and countless other options. One clever idea we love transforms a vintage printed tablecloth into colorful valances. It really brightens up the space!

You'll also appreciate the practical information scattered throughout *150 Ways to Dress Your Windows*: guidelines to help you estimate yardage, things to consider when working with patterns, and definitions of the technical terms you're likely to encounter in creating a window treatment. This expert advice helps you choose just the right materials at the fabric shop or home design store.

We're excited just thinking about the projects this book will inspire. Enjoy!

—The Editors of *Country Living*

Introduction

Windows are an essential architectural element—imagine how gloomy your home would be without them. Your appreciation of the light and air they admit and the view they provide may be intrinsic or, if you're house hunting or building, you may be giving windows a lot of thought. Aesthetically, most of us want windows to be something more than openings in the walls, and consider them an important element to be integrated with our decorating plan. Thus, we dress them accordingly—in formal attire or casual garb, as suits our style. The qualities that make windows wonderful also present challenges: Almost everyone wants a way to control the amount of natural light that enters a room and to mask the activities within from the eyes of people outside.

So many elements go into a window treatment—the style, fabric, color, and finishing details; the shape and size of the window; and your taste. How do you decide what will be right for you? One good way is to look at window treatments in other homes to find an interior you admire for its style or its similarity to your own home. Since you probably can't just knock on doors and must instead be an armchair voyeur, take your inspiration from the sets you see in films and on television and from the photos you find in magazines and books. Especially magazines and books about interior design—these provide insight into the designer's concepts, the materials used, or the technical considerations of the décor.

To give you ideas, *150 Ways to Dress Your Windows* is filled with photographs of classic and innovative window treatments. To put those ideas in context, the book is divided into two parts. The first, Elements of Style, discusses the various types of window fashion and reasons for choosing one style over another, how fabric can transform your window design and integrate it with your décor, and the fine details that make window treatments special. The second part, Window Fashions Room by Room, demonstrates the great versatility of window treatments—with examples organized by rooms of the house—and the role that they can play in creating a look you love.

8

Fuchsia, lime, tangerine, and red in dots, stripes, flowers, and checks comprise the major elements of this exuberant decorating scheme. The casings on the floor-length gingham curtains form a ruffle when the panels are condensed over the rods, a detail that makes this window treatment charming rather than old-fashioned. Spiral finials on the rods add to the fun.

PART ONE

ELEMENTS OF STYLE

Window fashions give character to a room much as a stylish outfit brings out the spirit of a person. Think of it this way: When dressing a window, you choose a garment shape—curtains, shades, or another type of treatment; a material—soft or crisp, plain or patterned; a color—one that flatters by day and by night; and then decide whether to add scarves or jewelry—trims such as fringe and ribbon, and hardware. What fun!

Whatever the size or shape of your window, and no matter which room it is in, you can start choosing its wardrobe by considering the style, fabric, and details that together will make it right for your décor. Chapters devoted to the options for each are in this section. Check out the possibilities; then turn to Part Two for more examples presented room by room.

LEFT White fabric, white walls, simple lines, and lovely light from large, evenly spaced windows: Plain, pleated curtains soften the background and let the landscape beyond be the real window treatment in this serene sitting room.

Choose a Style

How do you describe the character, or style, of the room you are ready to dress? Is it rustic, American traditional, sophisticated, a mix of flea market and vintage finds, or an entirely different interpretation of country style? Will the room be complemented by a formal window treatment or a casual approach, masses of heavy fabric or something slight and delicate? Will curves or pleats make the statement or will a flat design bring the right look? Do you wish the window treatment to be prominent or to blend with the walls? Will your fashions conceal a flaw or celebrate an asset?

Not sure how to answer? There are only four basic types of window treatments. Once you understand the benefits and drawbacks of each, and see that any one can be made in myriad fabrics and colors to give it the look you want, your decision about which to use will be easy.

Here's a brief summary of the four types of window treatments: Curtains and draperies are generous panels of fabric that hang from poles and can be pulled horizontally across the pole to cover or reveal the window. Shades and blinds may be constructed of fabric or another pliable material; they hang from poles or boards, and open or close vertically. Toppers, including valances, scarves, swags, and rigid cornices, cover the top portion of the window and are not adjustable. Shutters are rigid and hinged to the sides of the window recess. Blinds and some types of shutters have louvers that can be tilted to control the light. Each of these window treatments can be used alone or in combination with one or more of the others. Almost all of them may be mounted inside the window recess, a choice that leaves the molding trim on display, or mounted outside of the recess, which covers at least part of the molding. You'll see examples of all types, with many variations, throughout this book.

Roman shades are flat, flexible panels that fall into stacked horizontal pleats when they are raised. If there are dowels inserted behind the pleats, they will be crisp and tailored like these; without the dowels, they'll be soft and slightly draped—a style sometimes called relaxed. Framed by crisp white moldings and rich gray walls, these black-and-white toile print shades have a dressy yet slightly whimsical demeanor. If you prefer not to see the moldings, you can make Roman shades wider and mount them outside the window rather than inside, but they will stand away from the frame a bit, and you'll see a gap from the side.

A deep smocked border gives these otherwise plain white curtains a simple, feminine elegance that suits the bay window and vintage wallpaper. They're twisted around a pretty holdback to reveal the view. Sheer curtains don't provide any nighttime privacy or block sunlight and moonlight for those who wish to sleep in the dark, but in a coastal setting like this, it may not matter. (If it does, add a discreet roller shade to each window.)

The window in this small alcove could have easily been left bare, but the homeowner chose a simple Roman shade in a pale floral linen to soften the bright light pouring in. Linen drapes well, making it a good choice for either Roman shades or soft curtains.

A monochrome palette of soft golden hues in subtle patterns fills this bedroom with a restful glow, and silhouettes the elaborate bedstead. Plain curtains on rings give a gentle softness by day; when closed at night they create a cocoon. Brass rods with pretty finials add a dressy touch—they are mounted flush with the top of the window molding, which disappears when the curtains are closed.

This gathered valance adds a flourish to the windows behind the bed and sets off the pretty linens in a room almost totally covered in one eye-catching pattern. If you love a pattern that's as strong as this French country example, you can use a lot of it to great effect as long as you're judicious in your use of other textiles in the room. Here, the soft volume of the valance adds texture, yet blends with the walls and ceiling instead of distracting your eye. It conceals shades that can be lowered for privacy.

Curtains or Drapes?

We tend to use the terms *curtains* and *draperies* interchangeably, and that's fine for most purposes. But to a workroom there can be a difference, so if you are having them made, make sure you are clear about the construction. The top of a drapery panel is pleated or gathered before it is installed. Curtain panels are flat until they are hung. Both curtains and draperies can be lined or left unlined. Some curtains have a casing across the top that slides over the curtain rod. This type is difficult to push open; instead, these panels are usually tied back or draped over decorative hardware, called holdbacks, that is mounted at the side of the window. Both curtains and draperies can be attached to rings and hung from horizontal poles, which makes them easier to open and close, though tiebacks or holdbacks may still be used to keep them open.

Shutters painted to match the window trim are discreet and unobtrusive. Here, in pristine white against airy blue, they mask the lower portion of an alcove window; if you want full privacy, you could use a full-length version instead, or install another set in the top of the window. In a space where it's awkward to open the hinged panels, as it would be with the books, plant, and towels on this bench, louvered shutters are a smart idea: Just tilt the slats to admit more light. Of course, you'll have to open the panels if you want to raise the window.

Matchstick Roman shades are a natural choice for an informal beach house, and their sandy hue is a fine fit with sisal, sea grass, and blue-and-white nautical prints. These shades top a wall of sliding doors; to exit, you can pull up the shades or simply duck. And unlike curtains, when shades are completely open, they nearly disappear, taking no wall space when you want a clear view of the garden beyond.

Perhaps because they are reminiscent of a furled sail, informal roll-up fabric shades give a room a sporty finish. The one trimming this enclosed porch has a self-valance. If you prefer not to see the wrong side of the fabric on the roll, use a woven stripe, check, or solid that is the same on both sides.

In this casual country living room where a variety of patterns adorn the furniture, plain ivory cotton curtains accent the window against a rich yellow wall. These hang from self-ties on an iron rod, mounted right below the crown molding, and the treatment gets a fun accent from big wooden buttons sewn along the center opening. Curtains like these aren't easy to pull closed, especially when surrounded with furniture, so behind them, a bamboo Roman shade controlled by a cord can be lowered when privacy is desired.

Technical Terms

When you plan or shop for window treatments, you may run into some technical terms. Here are some definitions to help you converse like a pro.

Board-mounted: The treatment is stapled or glued to a board installed parallel to the floor across the top of the window. The board can be inside- or outside-mounted. Shades and swags are often board-mounted.

Casement: A window with the sash hinged on the side, usually opening out. French doors are big casement windows, usually opening in.

Double-hung: A window with two sashes, one above the other. One or both sashes slide up and down.

Inside mount: A treatment installed on a rod or board within the window recess, the same width as the sash. The window trim moldings are visible.

Leading edges: The vertical edges of curtains or draperies that meet in the middle of the window. These are the edges that move when the curtains are opened or closed.

Outside mount: A treatment installed on a rod or board attached to the wall outside the window recess. The window trim moldings are covered.

Overlap: The leading edges of draperies installed on tracks overlap at the middle of the window. You need to allow for this when you measure for the panel width.

Return: The distance from the front of a window treatment to the wall. Some treatments (especially board-mounted) are installed so they turn back to the wall and you cannot see behind them from the side. You need to include this distance when you measure.

Reveal: The depth of the window recess, from the face of the trim molding to the face of the sash (the face of the top sash if the window is double-hung). It can be difficult to install an inside-mounted treatment in a shallow reveal.

Rigging: A system of cords, usually threaded through rings sewn to the back of the treatment, by which a shade is raised and lowered.

Sash: The framed glass panels in a window. Each sash may contain one or more panes of glass.

Stackback: The wall space needed for curtains or draperies to fully expose the window when they are completely open. This is the distance from the inside edge of the window to the bracket holding the curtain rod or the end of the drapery track.

Choose a Fabric

Fabric, be it plain or patterned, colorful or subdued, brings endless potential to all the basic window fashions except shutters and louvered blinds. After all, most window treatments are just rectangles of fabric, sometimes flat, sometimes pleated or gathered, and they assume one personality in solid white, another in a vintage rose print, and yet another in bold stripes or in lace. Add to those possibilities options for the finish and weight—shiny, matte, velvety, homespun, smooth, crisp, soft, coarse, gauzy, or heavy, and you begin to see that "a curtain is a curtain" is not the case at all. When you're planning a window treatment, think about a style that will work for you, executed in a fabric that will make it come alive in your space.

Almost any kind of fabric can be used; the right choice depends on the look you want. Very heavy or stiff fabrics are seldom good options because they're difficult to manipulate, but some may work for large drapes, roller shades, a flat valance, or to upholster a cornice. Sheer fabrics don't provide privacy. Fragile fabrics may not wear well. Almost any fabric is prone to fading and sun damage over time—but chances are you'll get tired of it and replace it before it wears out. Informal, ready-made shades are commonly available in reed and split bamboo with a choice of various wood stains as well as colors, and also in synthetic materials, some of which have sun-blocking or thermal qualities. And if you love the idea of shutters and are wild for fabric, too, there are shutter frames that you can fill with the fabric of your choice.

If you are having window treatments made-to-order, or you are making them yourself, try to get a sizable swatch of any fabric you are considering so you can see the way it folds, pleats, and drapes, as well as check the color and pattern in the space where it will hang. If swatches are not available, it's worth purchasing a yard to play with before committing to a fabric. Even with a keen eye for design and a good sense of color, it can be difficult to visualize the effect of a particular material. One thing you can be sure of, the more there is of something, the more influence it will have on your overall décor. But don't worry, you're not the first person to dress a window, and there are lots of photos here and elsewhere that show different effects.

A lace panel makes a pretty café curtain and dresses up a plain space, providing some privacy, or masking an unappealing view. When hung flat like this one, the pattern stands in simple relief against the light; gathered lace would look more complicated. This panel was made by stitching together alternating lengths of four- and three-inch sturdy-weight cotton crochet trim. Lace is always a bit romantic, and there are many styles to be found; you can use new fabric or look for vintage pieces, which can be fun to mix and match.

the stars came out over the summer sea

Plain, lightweight fabric turns translucent when the sun's rays filter through it, casting each hem and fold into relief against the window and adding interest without introducing pattern or a change of color. Fine linen in a natural hue is an effective choice for a layered treatment like these cuffed curtains, which seem darker at the top because of the doubled fabric.

Prints are fun to mix when you're decorating, and one sure way to do so is to stick to a common color scheme while varying the scale of the motifs. Here, assorted blue-and-white patterns and a cushioned seat cozy up to a small, high window. Gathered curtains made in the large print put more white at the window than the small print would, making the window seem a bit bigger. Blue-and-white ball fringe adds a flourish to this charming spot.

Exuberant vine patterns based on traditional crewel embroidery make lively window treatments. They're available both embroidered and printed; either way, they're a fine choice for a home with a seventeenth-, eighteenth-, or early nineteenth-century flavor. Keep the look fresh by pairing this sort of print at the windows with solids on the furniture and some quieter patterns on the accessories.

Short curtains are not usually hung with a valance in such a formal shape, but here the effect is charming. The house is old, with lots of original and new period detail; the curtains are just one of the intriguing things that form a background for the rich wood hues and the lovely lines of the antique furnishings.

If you want to bring subtle interest to the picture, consider a textured fabric. There are all sorts, from ribbed chenille to coarsely woven monk's cloth, and each has its own charm. Quilted fabric says "comfort," and works nicely on upholstery, drapery, or cornices, so keep it in mind, especially if you enjoy decorating with textiles. These violet-and-plum toile curtains are lined with a quilted ivory fabric, making them reversible and also creating a border along the edges. The sofa is covered with the same quilted ivory fabric used to line the curtains.

Cleaning Tips

Dust and dirt in the air are inescapable facts of life. If you wish to clean your window treatments, consider two things: their size and the materials they're made of—including trims, lining, and hidden interfacings. Some informal treatments that are small and lightweight can be laundered, but many decorator fabrics have protective finishes that aren't meant to go through the washer and dryer, so always check the manufacturer's label. Large treatments are often too bulky to wash anyway. You can spot clean stains, vacuum dust (use a soft brush attachment), send the panels to the dry cleaner, or have a service come to your home to clean them. If you have your window treatments custom-made, keep some scraps of the fabric so you can test cleaning methods.

Shades, blinds, and shutters made of wood, reed, vinyl, or metal can be vacuumed and wiped with a damp cloth. If necessary, use a mild household cleanser to dissolve spots.

Bold horizontal stripes in two quiet but complementary tones accent the curtains on this window wall. Wide, uneven, and strategically positioned, stripes like these add interest without drama, and here they look informal, modern, and not at all fussy. You can sew two fabrics together to create this kind of stripe, or consider pairing a sheer fabric with one that's opaque, or a print with a solid.

Here, a simple black-and-white striped Roman shade mounted inside the window frame matches the fabric used on the seat of the chair. Mounting shades inside the frame allows the window frame to show, a good choice if you have decorative frames.

Estimating Yardage

Window treatments can require a lot of fabric, so it makes sense to have an idea of the yardage in order to budget realistically, or to know at a glance that the bargain bolt you're eyeing is sufficient for your needs. Precise planning takes careful measuring; if you are having the treatments made, your workroom should do this, or there are many good do-it-yourself books to guide you. Here is the rule of thumb for a quick estimate:

CALCULATING FOR PLAIN FABRIC

1. Determine the height of the wall space to be covered for one treatment (one curtain panel, one shade, one valance). Add 18 inches for hems and top finishing. This is the *cut length* of one panel.

2. Determine the width of the wall space to be covered (the window width plus however much the treatment extends to the sides). If the treatment is not flat, decide how full it will be (curtains, gathered valances, and gathered shades are usually two to three times the width of the wall space). If this figure is greater than the width of your fabric, you'll need two lengths of fabric for each panel. Determine how many lengths you need in total.

3. Multiply the cut length measurement by the number of lengths you need. Divide by 36 inches to find the total yards needed.

CALCULATING FOR PATTERNED FABRIC

If your fabric is patterned, find the length of the repeat (see page 37). Complete step 1 above. Divide the *cut length* by the repeat length and round up to the next whole number. This gives you the number of repeats required per length in order to make matching panels. Multiply the repeat length by the number of repeats needed to find the cut length per panel in your patterned fabric and proceed with steps 2 and 3 above.

For example, if the cut length is 80 inches and the repeat length is 24 inches: 80 ÷ 24 = 3.33; round up to see that you need 4 repeats per length. 4 x 24 = 96 inches, the cut length of one panel in the patterned fabric.

Moiré is an embossing technique accomplished with a heat press; it imparts a tone-on-tone wavy pattern that's subtle, elegant, and very classic. It's most often applied to shimmery silk or rayon fabrics woven with a fine horizontal rib, though you may find it on velvet and wool as well. There are also moiré prints, which do not catch the light in the same way. Moiré is especially suited to period décor, as here, where it has been lined in a contrast fabric and used for traditional pleated cascades, which fall from a swag draped across each window top.

Your first assessment of stripes may be that they give a tidy, regimented geometry to whatever they adorn, but use them for something that's not flat and they offer appealing surprises. When this cloud shade is lowered, the silk stripes shimmer and flute gently, but when it's raised, as here, they curve and billow most prettily. Keep the scale in mind when you play with stripes this way—small, regular stripes may appear as a single hue or may seem to vibrate, especially in a large room.

1, 2, 3: It's a Curtain

Curtains are one element of home décor that truly can be created by anyone. There's nothing that says sewing must be part of the picture, and least of all, sewing by machine. All you need is a length of fabric and an ingenious approach to hanging it. If it needs a hem, and that's not among your skills, look for an iron-on, double-sided tape (in the notions department of any general merchandise store) and follow the package directions. Here are a couple of clever ideas.

OPPOSITE PAGE
Clip artistry: Hang a wire curtain "rod" above your window—you can purchase these from home stores or rig your own from two closet hooks and some wire, or even cord. Raid an office- or beauty-supply store for good-looking hinged paper clips or hair clips. Fold the top of your fabric over the wire and clip in place at regular intervals. The fabric used for this panel is a suave damask secured with bulldog paper clips.

LEFT
Who's got the buttons? Install whatever type of curtain rod suits your look. To make a casing at the top of your curtain, simply fold over a margin of fabric a bit deeper than you need to slide over the rod and secure it by sewing buttons through both layers at regular intervals. Mother-of-pearl buttons dot the top of this sheer panel; consider flower-shaped buttons on a pretty print, antique Bakelite shapes on a novelty geometric, or something glittery on velvet or rich damask.

It hardly matters that yesterday's news isn't fabric: For the budget-conscious or those in need of a temporary topper, the classified section stands in handily for the real thing. If you're thinking long-term, reinforce the newsprint with iron-on interfacing. These scalloped valances are even decorated with dressy little tassels.

If you come across a summery picnic cloth that sports lavish bouquets in the corners, consider cutting it in half, mounting each piece as a valance, and pinning up the middle of each to create a double swag that shows the motifs and borders to advantage.

How cute is this? A whimsical tablecloth cut in half diagonally and edged with spunky ball fringe is charming atop a Roman shade made of narrow linen toweling.

Toile fabric lends formality to these crisp Roman shades. There's a medallion centered right below the self-valance, and as the shade pleats up, the motifs overlap to create a new, intriguing pattern.

Understanding Pattern Repeats

Almost all patterned fabrics have a motif that is repeated regularly over their surface. On a very small allover pattern, like tiny meandering ribbon or a petite floral calico, you are not usually aware of the unit of repetition. But for most patterns, it is easy to identify specific elements of the motif, which could be an isolated graphic, like a sailboat or bunch of cherries, or something loosely connected all over the surface—for instance, a bouquet with a rose in full bloom, a bud, and sprays of leaves arching left and right, all twined with ivy that merges into an identical bouquet. The measured distance from one spot on the motif—the tip of the sailboat's mast or the center of the full-blown rose—to the same spot on the next identical motif is called the repeat.

Most fabrics have both a vertical repeat and a horizontal one (stripes have one or the other, depending on how they're placed). A repeat is important in two ways: First, all but the smallest patterns need to be positioned thought-fully on the treatment, with like motifs placed at the same level on all treat-ments in a room, and matched at the seams. For example, plaids are usually planned so that the hem falls along a prominent stripe, but if a fabric has a large motif that doesn't repeat evenly over the length of the treatment, a full motif is placed at the top, where the eye will appreciate it, and a partial motif placed at the hem. The other important thing to remember about a repeat is that the larger the repeat and the more windows to be dressed, the more fabric you'll need in order to position and match the pattern properly (see page 30).

Choose the Details

Simple can be lovely, but what if your window fashions deserve a stylish finish? The world of ribbon, fringe, braid, and tassels is vast and enticing. You can use trims to accent the edges of your window treatment, choosing colors that match or contrast with the fabric. This is a good way to visually separate toppers from curtain panels made in the same fabric or to enhance the impact of a modest material or basic design. You can play with scale, sheen, and texture to create drama. You don't have to start from scratch to add trim either—if you can sew or use an iron-on adhesive, there's nothing to stop you from embellishing plain, off-the-shelf curtains or shades. And if your treatment incorporates visible hardware, your choice of poles, finials, and holdbacks can add color and sheen as well as design detail that's right for your décor. You can even find decorative pulls to trim your roller shades.

When considering trims, ready-made options such as fringe, ribbon, and lace come quickly to mind. But you can also add terrific detail with fabric, using either the same material as the body of your treatment or a contrasting fabric for binding, ruffles, or borders. In fact, if you are also having slipcovers or pillows made for your room, you can tie the look together by adding a bit of their fabric to your window treatment or vice versa.

Where to begin? Look at photos of interiors you like to see how designers use fringe, ribbon, braid, binding, ruffles, and the rest. Besides the choice of trim and the way it's used, consider two things: scale and budget. The size of your room and windows, the type of treatment, and the fabric used affect the scale of your window fashions. You don't want the details to be lost in the distance or the fabric pattern, so you can probably be a bit bolder than you would be when trimming a garment. Dollarwise, you're likely to need many yards of trim, which can put a dent in your budget. In fact, if deep heavy fringe or spectacular tassel tiebacks are a must, you may want to choose a modest fabric to balance their cost.

This elegant, two-color window treatment couldn't be much simpler: Silky scarlet fringe adds a graceful outline to the scalloped valance and the leading edge of the panel it tops. The lovely damask fabric has an understated pattern and the fringe shines against it. This classic design is somehow always formal, but you could lighten it up in plain muslin and matching cotton fringe, or even make it romantic in lace with lace edging.

Multicolor tassel fringe that picks up the hues of the fabric puts the prettiest edges on this classic swag, cascade, and curtain. The dressy rosettes accenting the top corners are more than decorative; they mask what could be a bulky arrangement of pleated layers. Maltese crosses (two crisscrossed loops of fabric or ribbon) and bows are other frequently used swag embellishments.

Use pretty lace to add a feminine touch to your window treatment. Here, two lace edgings, applied in three bands, grace a ready-made roller shade. You can often find vintage lace at flea markets (it's fine to cut it off worn linens) or look for new in a trimming store. Experiment to see how much contrast you like between lace and background: These laces are ecru and taupe against white; tone-on-tone is nice, too, as is lace against a ticking stripe.

Here's a room that stepped right out of a painting by beloved Swedish artist Carl Larsson. Bold cross-stitch embroidery borders simple muslin curtains that are tied with red-and-white gingham. Black iron rods with arrowhead finials help to focus your eye on the windows. A passion for handwork isn't necessary for replicating this look. You could begin with Scandinavian table linens, or you could find similar embroidered bands at trimming shops, or have someone with an embroidery machine make some for you.

Perennially charming ball fringe adds a jaunty edge to the length of red-and-white gingham tossed over holdbacks above this window. Three-quarter height, white shutters add privacy when needed and complete the dairy-fresh look.

Fringe in a tortoiseshell color softens the edge of these pleated silk curtains and complements the bamboo shade behind. Bamboo curtain rings and a fluted rod complete the look.

Short tabbed curtains are so traditional for an Early American–style home that they often go unnoticed. Here's a fresh take: The top, sides, and bottom are bordered with a slightly darker fabric (think velvet on muslin) and the long tabs are divided to resemble suspenders that fasten with covered buttons. This window and its trim molding are recessed, and the red curtain rod is mounted on the molding. Most homes don't have such thick walls; you can mount the rod on the molding anyway, or use a tension rod inside the window recess.

Hardware Details

Look through any home catalog or home store and you'll see dozens of options for curtain hardware. Even the rings that slide along the curtain rod have style. You can choose a quiet design or something with lots of character, so decide how much attention you want the hardware to call to itself. Then, look for a shape, color, finish, and scale that complements your room and fabric. If you're a flea-market devotee, search for vintage hardware that hints at history or reflects your favorite style—you never know what Lady Luck will send your way.

TOP RIGHT The pineapple finial—a classic Colonial decorative motif—picks up the deeper copper tone in the fabric and brings a gentle contrast to the wall. The curtain rods and rings, which are all made of bamboo with a tortoise-shell finish, lend a hint of the Far East to the window treatment.

RIGHT The curtain rod ends with plain ball finials; the dark bronze hardware complements the light colors on the wall and fabric. A simple ribbon with braided edges tailors the pretty rose print of this pleated panel. The full window treatment is on page 129.

CLOCKWISE FROM TOP LEFT

Holdbacks are like earrings or brooches for curtains. This pretty glass flower dresses up a quiet, meandering green-on-ecru pattern.

Nature doesn't do badly as a designer, and that's why she's so often imitated. This is the real thing: a branch rod resting in a bracket cut from the crook of a tree trunk—a clever idea for a rustic country home. The entire window treatment appears on page 152.

Favorite sports or hobbies can also inspire ideas for hardware. Here, in a room with angler-themed decorative touches, a battered oar that lost its mate has been given a surprising new role as a curtain rod, adding a touch of whimsy to this already charming window treatment.

When you're choosing window fashions, your first question should be, "What effect do I want to create in this room?" Choose the ambience you find pleasing and then decide which mix of design, fabric, and color will bring it to life. The considerations for living rooms, dining rooms, and bedrooms are similar, and chances are the windows play a fairly prominent role. You want to dress them in a way that enhances the space, and you probably need some degree of privacy as well. Window treatments for kitchens and bathrooms, while generally less involved than those in other rooms, make just as important a contribution to the décor and provide just as much opportunity for creative interpretation.

To start your thinking, take a tour of the rooms on the following pages. You'll see how similar window fashions have a different effect when used in rooms with dissimilar furnishings, and how the use of fabric, color, and finishing details alters the look and impact of the various treatment types. Keep your eye on combination treatments, where two or more components are used together to expand the design options and make the most of their effect. Which of the following rooms appeals most to you? Mark the page—you are well on your way to choosing the look that works for you.

LEFT For clean, contemporary style, choose curtains with huge grommets that will slide over a curtain pole. As you can see here, this makes the fabric fall in neat vertical folds and there are no rings to distract (or attract) your eye. When this type of curtain is closed, the pole appears to be laced through the top. The broad charcoal-brown stripe running across the middle of this white curtain adds graphic impact and ties into the color of the chair fabric and table bases without darkening the room.

Living Rooms

When choosing window treatments for a living room or sitting room, select a style and fabric that reflect the degree of formality or casualness with which you wish to surround your friends and family, choosing a look that is a fitting complement to your other furnishings. Be sure to give some thought to the time of day you most often use your living room—a room enjoyed for its natural light and view of the landscape may warrant a different treatment than one used mostly at night, when you might prefer to cover the window for privacy or coziness. The appearance of both fabric and color changes under different types of light, so you'll want to test samples by day and night to be sure they give the effect you're after. Perhaps one of the following rooms looks like the place where you'd like to entertain friends or curl up with a good book.

The medium stripe and unusual ceiling mount give this curtain a tailored look that suits the clean lines of this eclectically furnished room, where Asian pieces mix with modern and the walls wear a surprising moiré finish in robin's egg blue. Note how the stripes repeat the colors of the furnishings but not the walls, a choice that keeps your eye moving around the room. Because the rod curves up into the ceiling, this panel and its mate always frame the view—they can't be closed.

PART TWO: WINDOW FASHIONS ROOM BY ROOM

A deep, scalloped cornice puts a frame on these curtains, adding a touch of formality to this sitting room. The large, traditional floral-and-bird print is soft and pretty in tints of blue on an ivory ground. In a serious, period-style home, this window treatment would be "perfect"; here, it's kind of fun.

Look closely—ruffles soften the leading edges of the pleated panels on the double window at the back of this dressy room. The blue-on-white floral print is closely related to the toile covering the settee but doesn't match exactly, allowing each to hold its own. The curtain rod is mounted just below the crown molding, giving an illusion of greater height to the ceiling and taking attention away from the dissimilar height of the small window on the right.

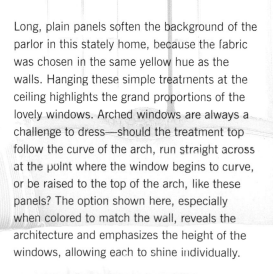

Long, plain panels soften the background of the parlor in this stately home, because the fabric was chosen in the same yellow hue as the walls. Hanging these simple treatments at the ceiling highlights the grand proportions of the lovely windows. Arched windows are always a challenge to dress—should the treatment top follow the curve of the arch, run straight across at the point where the window begins to curve, or be raised to the top of the arch, like these panels? The option shown here, especially when colored to match the wall, reveals the architecture and emphasizes the height of the windows, allowing each to shine individually.

If you prefer window treatments that won't interfere with the view or close in your space, opt for classic blinds like these. This sitting room is quite small and filled with petite yet amply curvy furniture; the blinds are tailored, add no bulk to the room, and do their job with discretion.

A CLOSER LOOK

Floral patterns are perfect for a country cottage, as seen in this weekend getaway home. Celery and rose hues are pretty and fresh on the traditional scalloped valance and curtains that frame the cottage's alcove window seat. The fabric features a floral bouquet in an offset, or *drop,* repeat, with the motif nicely centered on the valance.

1 The valance and curtains are fashioned from a fabric featuring a large-scale repeat. When designing a window treatment with a repeat, use the same principle you would when upholstering the furniture: Center the motif. Here, the bouquet pattern is centered on the valance.

2 The pink trim nicely accentuates the scalloped edge of the valance. The guideline for the ratio of valance to curtain length is one to five, but use your eye and the fabric pattern to adjust accordingly.

3 The floral motif is carried through on the pillows. Even though they feature a different print, it's still in the same family as the fabric used for the curtains and creates a harmonious mix.

4 The curtains puddle slightly on the floor. For a puddle effect, allow for at least three additional inches of fabric, more if you want a voluminous puddle.

ABOVE AND RIGHT

Roman shades of softly pleated linen in a natural hue let this assortment of fancy furniture breathe. The simply dressed windows allow you to view this tableau against the landscape, a backdrop that accentuates the charm of each unique piece.

Casement windows of twelve lights grace one wall of this room (above). The same linen Roman shade that's also used on the other wall looks more intimate here, and it's still a fine complement to the assorted treasures gathered nearby.

This room's blue-and-white country palette was inspired by the homeowner's collection of Cornish ware and Burleigh jugs. At the windows, a classic plaid looks snappy made up in pleated panels with tassel fringe for zest along the center edges. To mask the rigging cords, the white blinds behind the curtains feature vertical stripes sewn from the same plaid as the curtain fabric, but cleverly cut on the cross-grain to show only the smallest pattern repeats. Whitewashed granite walls create a bright backdrop for the pottery and layers of checks, plaids, and patchwork prints.

There's a reason plain white curtains are a popular choice for country-style decorating. They look fresh and uncomplicated—and who doesn't want to relax in a fresh, uncomplicated space? Here they repeat the color of the ceiling and moldings, make a simple frame for a large window, and enhance the airy calm of the décor. Behind them hang matchstick roll-up shades that repeat the honey tone of the floor.

If you are yearning for drama and don't wish to indulge it with voluminous draperies, consider this option: large but simple wood cornices, painted white like the window moldings, skirted with a muted plaid fabric and trimmed with a very fancy fringe. They top matching Roman shades. Everything's quiet and gently overscale here—tall windows, pictorial wallpaper, bold window treatments, and heraldic upholstery.

White cotton woven with a narrow vertical rib makes a crisp, fresh Roman shade that's perfect for the tall and narrow window in this pretty powder-blue sitting room. Made with dowels slipped into horizontal pockets on the back, this shade pleats up in neat folds. It's tailored but not at all severe—a sweet companion to the vintage fabrics on the settee and so discreet your eye can fully appreciate the floor-to-ceiling window.

The geometry of squares and stripes makes this an orderly room; it's softened by the pair of tufted armchairs and lots of plump pillows on the sofa. Louvered shutters give it a cool finish, filtering the bright sunlight into subtle stripes that complement the wallpaper and throw pillows. Architectural by nature, shutters are a fine choice here, where the windows are not the same: Curtains or billowing shades would call attention to the difference; instead, the unobtrusive panels covering the sash make a virtue of the exposed transom above the left window, and the louvers can be tilted to expose the view.

Everything old looks new again when it meets originality and a good design sense. This sitting room is in a thirteenth-century building in Tuscany; although the room's proportions are grand, the architecture is not ornate, making the simple, contemporary furnishings right at home. Very fine linen curtains hang from rings on rods set above the window recesses. Note how the deep brackets place the rods in front of the casement windows that open into the room. If you do have a stone house, you could keep this in mind when using both shutters and curtains.

Here's a softly dressed window that flatters but doesn't grab too much attention. Sheer, very full white curtains add a little froth to the quiet, casual comfort of this living room, while a translucent Roman shade picks up the ecru tones of the slipcovers and rug. Together, the shade and curtains filter light and, when closed at night, give a sense of privacy.

A CLOSER LOOK

When you're drawn to formal but don't want a heavy window treatment, consider using a top treatment alone, without matching curtain panels. Striped swags and cascades, hung high above a pair of French doors, give a light yet formal accent to this sitting room.

1 The tone-on-tone stripe is refined and restrained and not at all busy—a classic complement to the Federal chairs and dentil crown molding.

2 The dark piping outlining each swag and cascade is a nice touch, adding definition to the shapes and picking up the deep tones of the resident artist's still life paintings.

3 Here, the jabots hang from underneath the swag. See page 88 for an example of jabots hanging over the swag.

4 The doors are set in deep recesses where there's no room for curtain panels; the use of top treatments alone adds a soft touch and keeps the room airy and open to the garden.

A deep band of smocking gives a graceful finish to the top of these lightweight linen curtains. Linen possesses a natural stiffness, and the smocking brings some control to the volume here and seems more romantic than classic pinch pleats; it adds a pleasing, loose texture, too. These panels are mounted inside the windows to show off the lovely old moldings, which are painted white in contrast to the natural hues and black accents of the rest of the décor.

Panel shutters finish the windows in this room with an understated elegance that suits the surrounding moldings, which are broad but not ornate and feature a panel below the sill. The angular window treatment is a nice foil for the curvy details of the accessories. Bifold shutters like these hinge back on themselves, so you can fold back just the inner section for a semiprivate or shady effect.

With its monochrome pattern, toile is a great mixer. It has plenty of interest yet blends well with other fabrics. These billowing curtains are bordered with the same quilted fabric that covers the sofa. When paired with a rattan Roman shade, the window treatment relaxes the formal architecture and mixes comfortably with the stripes and checks covering the furniture. With big glass pocket doors being all that separates the rooms here, it makes sense that the library shares the palette of the sitting room and features the same window treatment.

Here are curtains chosen by someone for whom the
view is essential. If you need to close the curtains,
the grommets at the top slip over pegs on the window
molding. Although the curtains are not easy to adjust,
this is a minor consideration given the smart look they
bring to this informal sitting room—you can always
keep a step stool or a pole with a hook nearby.

Unexpected color turns these simple curtains into something special and makes you feel like it's always springtime in this room. The curtain panels are lined with the same gold fabric that covers those big cushy sofa pillows—and for a nice touch, the casing at the top, crushed over the curtain rods, is also gold. The hue of the panels is drawn into the room as the accent stripe on the upholstery.

Nuance is key to romance and this room has it right: layers of gold and amber, subtle patterns, accents of soft fringe, gracious proportions. At the window, two sets of curtains are hung—each on its own pole, so it can be closed independently. The inside curtain is a delicate scrim, with a turned-down cuff that drapes gently across the top. On the curtain in front, the satin weave gives a lovely sheen to the elegant damask, which is accented with a flat band of ribbon several inches from the top. It's the generous interval at which the rings are attached that gives this pair their lazy folds—the more space between rings, the more the fabric drapes when the rings are pushed together.

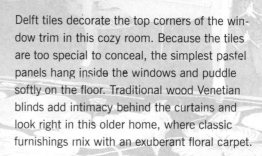

Delft tiles decorate the top corners of the window trim in this cozy room. Because the tiles are too special to conceal, the simplest pastel panels hang inside the windows and puddle softly on the floor. Traditional wood Venetian blinds add intimacy behind the curtains and look right in this older home, where classic furnishings mix with an exuberant floral carpet.

Period Dress

If you live in an old house, or one that replicates an older style, you may wish to use window fashions that are true to its architectural period. Somehow, swags and cascades that look very formal in a modern home tend to feel simpler in an old one, and quirky ruched or asymmetrical treatments that look odd or dated in a new house look totally charming when paired with the architecture they were designed for. It's not that these treatments are not good ideas for a new house, but it can be difficult to translate their proportions without changing their impact. Here are some ideas to consider.

In a house of modest proportions or one decorated in colonial-period style, minimal window treatments like these help a small room feel open and uncluttered and mix well with the simple lines of classic country furniture. In this room, the half-shutters with raised panels look snug and tie neatly with the dado. Simple scarf swags tossed over holdbacks at the top of each window soften the look and let in plenty of light. One caveat for shutters—they swing open into the room and may be awkward if left ajar.

In an old home with low ceilings, a top treatment alone may be all that's needed. These inside-mounted moiré swags are darling—they're structurally complex but perfectly proportioned and made in a fabric that's not busy.

Whether you offer tea or cocktails at a tavern table like this, it serves well for an intimate repast. It sits in an older home that's furnished in simple, period style. The fringed scarf topping the window suits the look, and fortunately, the house is situated where privacy is not a concern, so the topper is all that's needed. Anyone can replicate this look—the scarf is just a length of fabric draped over a pair of hold-backs affixed to the window molding.

Dining Rooms

In most dining rooms, the table and chairs take their traditional places in the center of the room, leaving the windows and their treatments in full view. For the sake of practicality, generations have equipped their dining rooms almost completely with unupholstered furniture, so it's likely the only other textiles in the room will be the table covering and perhaps a carpet. Even in homes where a section of the living room functions as the dining area, window treatments provide an opportunity for introducing texture, color, and pattern to space that might not otherwise have much: How important would you like these to be in your room and what effect would you like to create? Depending on your answer and your architecture, use window fashions as punctuation or as a backdrop, to create an ambience of dignified formality or a relaxed welcome, to enhance intimacy, or to celebrate a connection to the outdoors.

Roman shades made in a loosely woven, neutral-color fabric pleat softly in the tall windows of this sunny dining spot, which has a domed ceiling above a built-out molding. The shades are unassuming but effective, softening the daylight and gently complementing the assorted seating, striped rug, and collection of mid-1800s salt-glazed stoneware crocks.

Full-length, simple golden drapes, just a shade or so darker than the mellow paint, accent the end wall in this dining room. Notice the thoughtful choice of a rod that curves back to the wall, a design that gives the look of fullness without extending the drapes farther across the wall, and emphasizes the length of the drapes and the height of the room, too. The dressmaker details on the slipcovers follow the same plan of elegant understatement to perfect effect.

By daylight or candlelight, rich egg-yolk colors suffuse this room. At the window, a sheer curtain made from a light-catching sari offers delicate contrast to the intense hues inside. It hangs from a slender rod with a stylized leaf bracket.

Lots of windows, lots of light, and a leafy landscape combine with soft green walls and accents of red and yellow to make this a fresh and charming spot to take a meal. Plain white roller shades diffuse the sunlight and blend inconspicuously into the woodwork—you don't really notice them, but without their gentle influence, this room wouldn't feel nearly as serene. The design of the shades is ingenious: They are mounted at the windowsills and pull up through pulleys at the top. The result is privacy that doesn't hide the sky. Silver-plated tin charms were converted into decorative shade pulls.

Crisp Roman shades in a translucent material give a
modern finish that suits the contemporary furnishings of
this dining area. These are mounted inside the window
molding, so whether they're up or down, the rhythm
of the architecture is not obscured. They have a self-
valance and when fully raised, you hardly notice them.

Plain, lightweight linen shades drawn up into graceful curves dress the windows in this farmhouse dining room. These Roman shades are made without dowels and rigged with cords at the sides and in the middle; if the middle cord were omitted, there would be only one pouf per shade.

An understated window treatment lets all of your other furnishings shine. This discreet hand-sewn linen curtain, sill-length and hung inside the molding, makes the window look finished but adds no weight. A small brass knob holds the matching tieback. This is a simple and pretty choice that complements the delicate furniture and the collection of soft-paste pearlware.

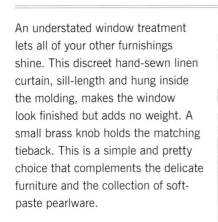

A CLOSER LOOK

If you want to dress your windows in soft volume that doesn't overwhelm, use a gathered cloud shade, or its pleated cousin, a balloon shade.

1 Billowing cloud shades provide graceful cover for these wide windows, where either full-length curtains or a flat treatment would emphasize their proportions and might look too plain.

2 Raised by cords running through rings on the back, cloud shades are similar to Roman shades, but they are gathered across the top; when the shade is raised, the fabric falls into a swag between every pair of cords.

3 Striped taffeta fabric emphasizes the draping and always makes a cloud shade especially lively.

4 These shades are rigged with just two cords, which are inset from the edges so that the sides hang down in a fan shape and the center swag becomes quite wide.

Coordinated but not-quite-matching window treatments create a lively backdrop in this small dining area. On the side walls, plaid cornices top cream-and-rose floral curtains and lead the eye toward the French doors at the back, where darker curtains on rings are bordered with the same plaid. The simple pole across the peaked wall keeps the effect open and light.

This New England farmhouse has been returned to its nineteenth-century roots and filled with colorful Early American antiques. The fabric used here (found in an antiques shop) features a pink toile combined with aubergine images of sixteenth- and seventeenth-century historical European figures. The rag-painted wall treatment with faux marbre band repeats the palette of the print to create a harmonious whole.

Worn paint, antique silver, old lace, and an eccentric wire chair—such romantic elements warrant a charming window treatment. This tie-up valance is just the right mix of casual and fancy. It's made from a tone-on-tone cotton with a swirl pattern, trimmed with tassel fringe, and mounted right on the sash, so the vintage casement window can swing in. Tie-ups are similar to Roman shades but they are not adjustable; they're folded up by hand and cradled by ribbons tied in bows.

Upon entering this room our immediate impression is that of a lovely porch scene from yesteryear, but actually it's a sunny room set up to look as though it awaits a garden party, with ornate wicker armchairs gathered around a table, a stylized flower chandelier, and lots of summery vintage fabrics. Softening the window in the back wall is a long lace curtain, mounted on a tension rod below the window top and floating down over the sill to the floor.

When wall space is limited, consider hanging a window treatment inside the window. This small dining area is right inside the entry door and is blessed with a built-in cupboard that makes for great display but, with its doors ajar, bumps right into the window on the adjacent wall. Luckily, the walls are thick here, the cupboard door fits into the window recess, and the deep sill offers more display space. All that's needed to trim the window is a valance made from a piece of pretty lace.

The paint color calls attention to the window sash in a room where all the other moldings are pure white. The black beautifully outlines each pane of the divided glass, and it picks up the black of the dining chairs as well. Folded back against the wall the louvered shutters in finished wood pivot on specialty hinges, allowing them to be mounted directly on the window casings.

Pristine white can be as pretty as a picture: Demure skirted
chairs, an array of plump pillows in the back, and soft
Roman shades—one per double window—look fresh and
inviting against the white floor, walls, and ceiling. Imbued
with Scandinavian style, it's a lovely spot for dining.

Thick stone walls create deep-set windows, which are perfect candidates for shutters. In this room, the meeting of the rustic with the refined creates a singular pleasure, as dressy accoutrements contrast with rough walls and simple painted woodwork. The shutters fold back into the window recess, adding a little texture but basically disappearing until needed for shade or privacy.

A CLOSER LOOK

Loving hands restored this Bucks County, Pennsylvania, stone house to its original glory and furnished it with a mix of European and American antiques. The window treatment framing the 12-over-12 windows is a classic approach for such a gracious dining room.

1 The valances are made from antique silk, with jabots that fall over the swags (as opposed to falling under the swags, as seen on page 62).

2 Fabric tiebacks secure the silk curtains, creating a graceful swoop.

3 Gold tassel fringe outlines the swag and jabots, picking up the gold in the tiebacks.

4 The curtains are made from a contemporary ivory silk that hangs in elegant folds below the tiebacks.

Pretty fabric is all it takes to bring a quiet room to life; in this dining room, the vivid color and classic floral print of the draperies call attention to the French doors and the view beyond. After the vista vanishes with the setting sun, the draperies make a warm backdrop when closed at night. Red and green are complementary colors (opposites on the color wheel), and while complements are often jazzy, the intensity of these colors varies so the effect is restrained. The green is soft and muted while the red is strong but tempered by green-and-gold floral motifs.

Color and pattern tell the story in this dining room and kitchen combo: Blue and yellow with white; big checks, and a scenic toile show this homeowner's love for all things French Country. The drapes hang ceiling-to-floor, bringing much-needed vertical lines to the long, low room; they ride on classic tracks, with cords behind the fabric to pull them open or closed. Matching short curtains hang over the counter on the back wall in the kitchen area.

Swags with cascades add to the fun in this charming octagonal summer room, where red and black travel from floor to chairs to chandelier. The draped shapes offer a festive complement to the exposed rafters, and you can't help but smile at the bright color. Note how the swags are shallow and mounted high above the window transoms so as not to interfere with the doors.

Kitchens

Cooking is a messy art, and neither splatters nor steam is good for fabric, so it's little wonder that people often choose top treatments or simple shades or blinds to dress a kitchen window. Besides, most kitchen windows compete with cabinets or display shelves for attention, and fussy treatments tend to look either crowded or dowdy. Privacy is often of less concern in a kitchen than in other rooms, but this depends on your location. If a top treatment alone is not sufficient for you and decorative shades don't appeal, a plain roller shade or mini-blind can provide privacy unobtrusively (both will tuck under a more decorative valance when not needed). If a kitchen has several windows of different sizes or in different work areas, they need not be dressed identically as long as the treatments share fabric or color or relate in some other way. If the kitchen is open to another room, consider using the same fabric for the window treatments in both.

Some windows look their best wearing nothing but a little old-fashioned lace. In this kitchen, the salvaged cupboards and general aura of days gone by call for a bit of antique finery at the windows. These mismatched lengths of lace came from the homeowner's collection of textiles.

Tie-up valances provide just the right mix of tailored and soft to balance the two strong, contrasting elements that frame this double window: tall wainscoting in beadboard and bold wallpaper patterned with roosters in fancy frames. Small brown-and-cream stripes are the perfect choice for the fabric. Toppers that have a hand-rolled lower edge cradled by ribbon ties like this are sometimes called stagecoach valances—a name in keeping with the nostalgic charm of this kitchen.

This window has no top or side molding, so an inside-mounted, flat window treatment like this bamboo Roman shade complements the plain architecture while ceding attention to the oversize shelves. These bamboo shades are inexpensive and widely available in both Roman and roll-up styles; the natural color of this one provides just enough contrast to the wall to be interesting but not intrusive.

Who doesn't love to lunch in a big country kitchen? If you're lucky enough to have a spot like this, consider dressing the windows informally in fun café curtains. This cheerful set is made in a tablecloth check, pleated at the top, and hung on tension rods inside the windows.

Fruit-punch colors give vintage charm to this large kitchen. The yellow board wall sports a bright red window next to a grass-green cupboard, and the tablecloth matches all three hues. Tied over the window is a white cotton curtain with crochet trim along the side; it's draped casually through a spiral metal holdback and cascades from there midway to the floor.

Corner windows truly expand your horizon. This one is large and, left unadorned, might seem to float under the raised ceiling. Keeping it anchored while maintaining its panoramic virtues are a set of toile swags at the top and fresh white café curtains across the bottom. Add lots of blue and white, a display of antique china, handsome cabinets, a big island, and a gentle breeze to create a classic country kitchen.

A CLOSER LOOK

Top treatments are often the finish of choice for kitchen windows because they don't get in the way.

1 A bay window can be a challenge to decorate. You'll have to consider whether you want to fit each individual window with a treatment or unite the windows by running a valance across all, or, as seen here, install the treatment outside the wall.

2 The red-and-white print fabric adds country cheer to complement the black-and-white checkerboard tiles. You can't go wrong with a bit of red in a white kitchen—it's classic, and it warms the coolness that sometimes fills an all-white space.

3 Open at the top, pole swags are graceful and visually lighter than their board-mounted cousins. They look as if they're just tossed over the pole, but don't count on that—most are made of individual, carefully pleated components that are held in place with staples or Velcro.

Ordinary muslin makes a casual, country-style window treatment in this unassuming beach house kitchen that captures the mood perfectly of lazy summer days spent at the seashore. The quirky Roman shade has a casing at the top that gathers ever so slightly over a U-shaped curtain rod that's narrower than the window trim.

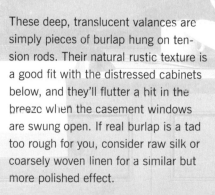

These deep, translucent valances are simply pieces of burlap hung on tension rods. Their natural rustic texture is a good fit with the distressed cabinets below, and they'll flutter a bit in the breeze when the casement windows are swung open. If real burlap is a tad too rough for you, consider raw silk or coarsely woven linen for a similar but more polished effect.

A striped, flat valance brings some warmth to the top of the window recess in this apartment kitchen and moderates the extreme vertical impact of a tall window in such a compact space. The simple style of the valance works well with the sleek cabinets; all the stripes (note the light fixture) and the brown transferware add personality. Hung behind the valance, a fully lowered, sheer white shade screens the view.

This sun-filled cottage kitchen is graced with multiple tall casement windows, each dressed in a neutral-colored blind that gives emphasis to the elegant architectural lines of the windows. Each blind can be drawn or lowered individually, allowing for maximum control over light and privacy.

A CLOSER LOOK

This spacious kitchen is blessed with a high ceiling and two very tall windows, perfect for Roman shades. A flatter treatment like a roller shade would work here, too, but these relaxed shades are more interesting, and their casual pleats fit perfectly in the country ambience of this kitchen.

1 The white Roman shades look soft and pretty without calling attention to themselves, and help bring coziness to the tall windows.

2 The rigging system on these shades creates loose folds, adding some texture and softness to a room that is filled with stainless steel, pottery, subway tiles, and other hard surfaces.

3 When raised as they are here, the shades extend the horizontal line of the shelf of white ironstone china.

Matchstick roll-up shades look as sophisticated as anyone could want in this contemporary beach house kitchen. Hues of sea, sun, and sand mix with bright white here; the ready-made shades mean no fuss, and swing nonchalantly in the three windows recessed at the back.

Bathrooms

While privacy is often of principal concern when a bathroom window treatment is chosen, the style of your bathroom—whatever it may be—gives you an excellent excuse to add a chic finish to the windows: Since every fixture and fitting, the tile, and the colors have been chosen with care, why stop there? Simple treatments like shutters, roller shades, or blinds will be easiest to care for, but unless the window is adjacent to the tub or above the sink, or there is no danger of damage from the steam from the shower, you need not limit your design choices. Instead, think about the ambience and the proportions of the room—is your bath glamorous, intimate, rustic, quaint, retro, or sleekly modern? Are the ceilings high or low, the windows petite or grand? Are you looking for the drama of swept-back draperies in luxurious fabric, or something crisp and fresh, or something whimsical? Decide, and then go for it. The only caveat: Choose towels that complement the style.

Antique linens provide a fitting finish to the window in this old-fashioned bath, where board wainscoting and sweet floral-stripe wallpaper show off a stenciled claw-foot tub and wire accessories add a touch of whimsy. To cover the lower window sash, a new curtain rod with clear-glass finials has been mounted on the molding; draped over it is a small table cover with embroidered corners, topped with a piece of filet crochet. Small tassels weight the corners of the cloth. A plain white shower curtain completes the look; note the buttoned-on border at its hem.

This intimate tub alcove offers a delightful place for a contemplative soak. It's beautifully appointed, the chandelier is fun by day and a treat at night, and the bank of windows offers fresh air, light, and a pretty prospect. Natural light is such a pleasure in a bathroom, but leaving windows bare so you can enjoy it is not always possible. Louvered shutters can provide privacy, and they bring a satisfying tidiness to the room, too. Louvered shutters are easy to clean, making them a great choice for a bathroom.

Swag or shade? The name doesn't matter when the shipshape look is just right. Mounted on the high, awning window above this tub is a flat cloth: Grommets in the top corners hook onto the molding and the center of the bottom hem is also hooked up to the top; that's what creates the swag effect. This sail-inspired, tailored window treatment adds visual interest that suits the seaside theme of the décor.

Soakers lounging in this deep tub can enjoy both privacy and sunlight thanks to top-down/bottom-up Roman shades, which can be lowered to expose the top window sash while keeping the lower one covered or be operated in the usual way. The natural linen works well with the taupe walls and the spare design is both classic and stylish, like the ambience.

Simple accoutrements give this modest bath a fresh, clean appeal: Small blue tiles on the tub surround evoke the ocean, a whimsical arrangement of shells decorates a table, and almost everything else is pristine and white. Attracting almost no attention at the windows are ready-made white bamboo Roman shades with a self-valance—no fuss, no clutter, and easy to raise and lower.

A CLOSER LOOK

This small bathroom reflects elements of the French country style the homeowner holds dear. It's remarkable for the shell-encrusted trim between the tile and beadboard and the shell-embellished chandelier. Adding a little country romance at the window is a pretty gingham-check cloud shade and a short, pleated white curtain with a toile border.

1 The blue-and-white colors of the buffalo-plaid cloud shade carry the seashore theme of the bathroom's décor onto the window treatment.

2 Cream-colored French linen curtains act as a frame for the cloud shade.

3 The linen curtains are trimmed with blue-and-white toile fabric. The patterns work together because they're in the same color family.

4 The cloud shade has a short "header," or a small amount of fabric that extends above the rod pocket. This simple feature creates a row of diminutive ruffles across the top of the treatment, softening the straight line of the rod.

This peaked-ceiling alcove with a small window makes a cozy setting for a relaxing bubble bath. The dark floor is a nice foil for the mix of white and ecru hues; together with the simple shutter on the window, they establish a sense of soothing calm. If curiosity overcomes you while bathing, just tilt those louvers for a glimpse of the outside.

Plain windows in a room with such glam exoticism simply wouldn't do. Full, floor-length curtains made in a small, allover geometric print balance the zebra-stripe rug, furry stool, and dressy classical furniture; inside the curtains (and easy to close without interference from the tub filler) hang roller shades with big ring pulls. A slender curtain rod is a nice choice here; it's in scale with the fabric print and doesn't call undue attention to itself.

Classic, overblown rose prints imbued with a vintage chic and combined with lots of eclectic textures prove that a bathroom doesn't have to have sleek, hard surfaces. These cotton curtains were acquired at an antiques fair and get their relaxed look from a turned-down top edge, created by rings attached to the back a few inches below the edge, and a holdback that catches the drapery on the side. A shirred sink skirt in a companion print hides the pipes under the sink and offers storage, too.

Who wouldn't love to primp at this feminine dressing table? A damask balloon shade adds an exuberant flourish above the skirted table, which is generously draped and trimmed with tassels. Pairs of vertical box pleats secured at the top fall open when the shade is raised and give it lots of sumptuous volume.

Woven roller shades in the windows cede prominence to the architecture in this inviting tub alcove, which offers the amenity of recessed shelves for towels and toiletries and is trimmed with tall wainscoting and handsome moldings. The translucent fabric echoes the wall color and casts soft, serene light into the room.

A CLOSER LOOK

Older homes sometimes have the quirkiest bathrooms. This marigold attic setting in a Nantucket home overflows with quaint charm and warmth and needs only the simplest of window treatments.

1 A white vintage linen is reinvented as a charming curtain.

2 Curtain clips hung on a line make it easy to pull the linen panel aside to let more light in.

3 Another line is strung above the tub to keep a bath towel at hand.

Masculine meets feminine in this beach house bath, where tailored vanities with decorative hinges and marble tops support pretty blue glass bowl sinks, the traditional inset medicine cabinets are dark to match the vanities, and the old-fashioned tub has a watery blue exterior. A woven-reed Roman shade balances the dark and light extremes and gives a classic finish to the window. Sailing enthusiasts: Check out the lampshades.

Fair skies or cloudy, there's no way to miss the morning sunshine here. At the window tops hang short striped valances that seem demure against the exuberant grid painted freehand on the walls; one set of paneled shutters with cute crescent-moon cutouts provides privacy when needed. Bold black-and-white tiles form a checkerboard on the floor to anchor all the good cheer.

White marble, fabric, and wood unite elegantly in this serene master bath, where two sets of shutters filter sunlight and provide privacy. Functional and stylish, the shutters echo the shutterlike design on the bathroom doors, too.

Old house, old-fashioned tub, rich, earthy colors:
Here's a soothing spot for a relaxing soak. Stained
to match the window frame, the wide plank shutters
can swing closed over the tub rim when a bather
wants seclusion. Their simplicity suits the spare
look created by the board walls and ceiling and the
polished wood floor.

You can pamper your mind as well as your body in this beautifully detailed bathroom retreat. The handsome, glowing paneling and built-in cushioned banquette give the room a quiet elegance, suggesting the solitude of a library or den, and the fittings share the refined aesthetic. Classic Venetian blinds in wood provide the perfectly discreet window covering.

Leaving Windows Bare

With their color, texture, volume, and style, window treatments contribute greatly to the ambience of a room. What if you omit them altogether? The window architecture will be more prominent and the room may feel larger or more open. If the windows are trimmed with molding, you can show it off—paint the molding to contrast with the walls for graphic impact or paint it to match for a calm sophistication. Fine wood moldings that are stained and finished will offer classic elegance that begs to be seen. Bare windows make the view more important and increase the natural light inside. One caveat: Undressed windows can look stark or even cold, especially at night, but this depends on the style of the window, the surrounding moldings, and the depth of the window recess. Of course, the choice is yours; the only reason you "must" use a window treatment is to provide privacy. Consider these examples of bare windows.

OPPOSITE PAGE The office and studio of an interior designer, this room is distinguished by the contrast of a snow-white ceiling and moldings against very dark, gray-green walls and floor. The window draws your eye, the furnishings are spare, and the overall mood is one of discipline and quiet, with—in this pretty light—a bit of mystery, too.

THIS PAGE, CLOCKWISE FROM TOP LEFT
Windows stretching from the floor nearly to the ceiling, with molding painted to match the walls and the glass unobscured, lend a conservatory feeling to this simply furnished sitting room.

The bank of awning windows above this bed lets in lots of light. Individually, the windows are small, but as a group, they fill a wide, shallow space. Adding a covering would make their proportions awkward and spoil the daylight.

Woodwork and walls in mellow, contrasting colors unite the architectural details of this room, surrounding the antique furnishings with an interesting frame that would lose its rhythm if there were cloth at the windows.

Bedrooms

Everyone has a personal notion of the ideal look for a bedroom. Romantic, tailored, opulent, spare, cozy as a cocoon, open as the sky—all these and more are options, and there are window treatments to enhance every choice. If you choose a fabric window treatment, you have the option of coordinating it with your bed linens or any upholstery in the room; if you frequently change the spread or coverlet topping your bed, you'll want to bear that in mind when dressing the windows. Key point: Include a room-darkening component if you prefer not to slumber with moonbeams and sunlight.

Cloud shades of blue-and-yellow toile mounted at the ceiling pull up into lush poufs and disguise the fact that the windows are set in the wall at different heights. When shades like these are lowered, the gathered fabric hangs straight, like a big curtain. This treatment can also be made as a valance, with the poufs permanently tied up. The longer the panel before it's rigged, the plumper the poufs will be, and if there is no rigging at the sides, the lower edge will turn into a fan shape at each end (see page 79 for an example).

Plain white blinds make a discreet window dressing for a bedroom where neat, low key, and pretty mingle as equals. Here the windows offer uncluttered light and air to a palette of sky and delphinium blues mixed with white. Take a practical look, too: These windows nearly meet in the corner, a setup that's hard to dress with curtains. Roman or roller shades would work as alternatives to blinds in windows like these, but they lack the tilting louvers that permit light and air to enter when the blinds are down.

Built-out corners at the end of this room and a window set in the middle of the space between them create a recess that's challenging to dress. Draperies spanning the space unify it, obscuring the small amount of wall on each side of the window and keeping the focus on the view. Just a few tones deeper than the walls, the gold-hued fabric looks rich and makes a subtle contrast; it's trimmed with matching tassel fringe. Soft Roman shades inside the window complete the effect and are easy to close—a boon since the cabinet under the window interferes with the drapes.

This bedroom is graced with a small alcove with floor-to-ceiling windows. When lowered, the Roman shades in the alcove extend to the floor to cover the tall windows. Because the shades are so long, there's lots of fabric to pull up, which makes them look luxurious and rather romantic when raised. Note how they're mounted on the window molding and meet in the alcove corners—there's no molding visible between them so they look like one big shade. Also, because they're outside-mounted, each shade is wide enough to "return" to the window; this extra width adds to the lovely draped effect.

Very full, crisp silk curtains crushed on their poles soften the walls of this bedroom, their billowing form echoing the contours of the upholstered bed and armchairs. The dark curtain poles with their dramatic finials and the sleek lines of the bed and chair frames take form against the creamy neutral tones and good natural light that give the room a serene glow. Curtains structured like these don't pull closed easily. Instead, in this room louvered shutters in the window next to the bed provide privacy when needed; the doors lead to a secluded garden.

The carved bed frame, elaborate pendant lamp, and antique picture frame are the first things to catch [...] this rustic bedroom in an 1[...] windows, humb[...] clean-lined lo[...] home's anti[...] finish pair[...] wainsco[...]

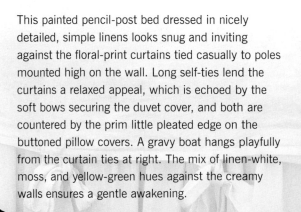

This painted pencil-post bed dressed in nicely detailed, simple linens looks snug and inviting against the floral-print curtains tied casually to poles mounted high on the wall. Long self-ties lend the curtains a relaxed appeal, which is echoed by the soft bows securing the duvet cover, and both are countered by the prim little pleated edge on the buttoned pillow covers. A gravy boat hangs playfully from the curtain ties at right. The mix of linen-white, moss, and yellow-green hues against the creamy walls ensures a gentle awakening.

A CLOSER LOOK

An assortment of fabrics in this room creates a pleasing mix. The button-tufted headboard, paisley bolster, and linen and ticking-striped pillow shams work comfortably together with the floral curtains.

1 To add drama to the room, the curtains were hung four inches above the window frame. Dark bronze hardware ties into the dark wood furniture.

2 Bamboo shades help control light during the day and keep the room dark at night.

3 Pinch-pleats on the curtains are sewn to the rings and add a touch of tailoring to the overall look.

4 Pale blue ribbon—the color choice was inspired by the blue background of the curtain fabric—was sewn onto the curtains as a trim. Seen from a distance, the soft floral print appears less distinct, and the ribbon gives definition to the treatment.

A whimsical print of dogs adorning fancy furnishings gives lots of
charm to these Roman shades and is right in keeping with the gently
eclectic décor in this bedroom, where a shared palette and graceful
lines keep everything working together. The shades are not fussy,
they're great for light control, and in this print, they make a nice,
unexpected accent that is appreciated even more at night when the
garden can't steal the scene.

The French are known to have a flair for style. With a mix of toile, check, and floral prints; pretty furniture; and an ornate mirror used as a headboard, that style translates happily to this feminine bedroom. Hanging side by side on a single pole above the window are two different curtains—a clever idea worth remembering whether you're shopping for ready-made or custom window fashions. A short inner panel would be easy to close above a bench or table, while the long one frames the outside.

A narrow dormer window is easy to overdress, producing a cluttered result, so flat shades or curtains with minimal volume are a good idea if you wish to maintain an open feeling. Here's a charming way to make a fashion statement and keep it under control: modest curtain; bold, witty motif. This stylized urn overflowing with fruit is especially nice against the subtle patterns and soft hues used throughout the room.

Privacy and Light Control

Transparency—the quality that makes windows such a delight—sometimes makes them problematic as well. The view inside can be as enticing as the view outside, so it's more comfortable, or even smart, to limit the exposure of the activities and contents within to both casual passersby and unduly curious eyes. Moreover, glare and heat from the sun can make a room unpleasant and, for most people, makes sleeping difficult. Bright sun is tough on textiles, too, causing fading and, in fragile fabrics, brittleness. Here are ways to meet the challenge:

Choose the right treatment: Most privacy- and light-control issues can be easily resolved if you plan from the outset to use an adjustable window treatment—one that can be drawn on and off the window, or raised and lowered, or tilted. If you use a top treatment (such as a valance or swag) without companion curtains, or a stationary one (such as curtains that don't slide easily over their pole or lose their aesthetic impact if released from their holdbacks), incorporate a second item (such as a roller shade or a blind) that is easy to operate, inconspicuous when not in use, and attractive when in view.

Get the right protection: There are various special materials that resolve issues of glare or unwanted translucency. If you want to enjoy a view from a room that gets too much sun, consider solar shades—you can see out through them, but they cut glare and protect against damage from ultraviolet light. If ambient light is a problem in a bedroom, there are blackout materials that can be used for linings or as shades. If your principal concern is preventing others from seeing in, remember that many fabrics (including some woven reeds) are translucent, or even transparent, when backlit. This means that when you turn on the lights in a room, anyone outside sees your window as a television screen, displaying all the action inside. To prevent this, line your window treatment or supplement it with a second component that is truly opaque.

Determine the right balance: Before totally shrouding all your windows, decide which really require a shield. Consider the locale in which you live, the activities for which each room is used, the floor where the room is located (upper-story rooms may be less exposed to neighbors and passersby), and the degree of opacity required. If you plan to close the treatments by day or if the exterior is lit at night, take a minute to think about the color of lining fabrics (or the wrong side of unlined treatments) or of bamboo, wood, or similar materials. It's usually more elegant if all the treatments in a home appear the same color from the outside. You don't want them to clash with the house's exterior either.

This small window is one of a pair whose high placement perfectly frames a headboard. When the furnishings are part vintage, part Swedish country, as here, the effect is all charm. In the window is a flirty little striped curtain with a crisp white hem; it's mounted on the lower sash, so it travels with the sash when the window is opened.

Dressed in pastels and floral prints, this room promises deep reveries by day and night. Long curtains covered in faded primroses make a nostalgic frame for the painted iron daybed, while fresher posies brighten the pillow. Notice the bed skirt hanging over the bed frame—it's made from dinner napkins tucked between the mattress and the frame.

Long white sheers set the stage for this bedroom that also functions as a sitting room, and they look just right for either role. For a modern touch in this older apartment, they're trimmed with a narrow blue ribbon and informally hung from clip-rings that ride on a wire rod. Blinds inside the window recess provide privacy when needed.

Black and white are a sophisticated pair, but they can be lighthearted, too. The spread and shams on this iron bed sport a nostalgic print of silhouette scenes surrounded by fancy topstitching that is reminiscent of old lace. The window is dressed in a classic shirting stripe whipped up as a curtain and tied to its pole with narrow black ribbons. The cool metal of the hardware plays off the room's gray-blue walls. For privacy, just reach behind the pillows and gently pull the curtain closed.

This modular home was inspired by classic American architecture and features two-over-two windows to give the dwelling a farmhouse feel. Tailored Roman shades in a black-and-white toile print enhance the cool serenity of the bedroom, where white moldings and ceiling accent the quiet backdrop of subdued blue walls and the rich walnut of the wide-plank floor. The black-and-white toile puts the dark accents of the armchair, picture frames, and other accessories in balance with the white linens.

There's something magical about sleeping under the eaves; perhaps it's a childhood memory or a vision from a beloved book that makes us happy to slumber in a room like this. A deep band of smocking gives an old-fashioned nightdress finish to the gauzy curtains, which float demurely next to the vintage floral wallpaper. The blue-and-white hues convey a fresh coastal mood at this Maine cottage.

Ideas for Peaked Ceilings

Dressing a window in a dormer or under a peaked ceiling can be a challenge. Sometimes there's not enough room for panels to pull completely away from the glass, and sometimes the proportions of the space just look unbalanced when a triangle of wall sits above a lot of fabric. Here are a few good solutions.

Gathered panels stapled to covered boards follow the peak in this attic bedroom. Made in a print fabric that picks up the wall color and swagged back with matching ties, they seem to curtsy below the contrasting ceiling.

ABOVE The exposed framing of this crafter's studio has plenty of interest; with everything painted white, the studs and rafters create a nice texture that draws your eye up and makes the room look bigger than it is. Inexpensive roll-up matchstick shades cut the glare and don't compete.

LEFT Swing-out curtain rods and thoughtfully chosen colors make a virtue of dormers cut just large enough to house the tall windows flanking this bed. The window frame is painted red, matching the red that appears on the drapes, quilt, and bed frame.

Great colors, charming collections, and an aged rope bed topped with bright linens: If you have a soft spot for country primitives, you'll see much to admire here. A simple windowpane-check cotton makes classic curtains for the deep-set window; note how the window recess is painted to match the chair rail and baseboard, but there's only the thinnest molding to outline it.

In this farmhouse guest room, raised-panel shutters on the lower half of each window are true to the Early American architecture. Since the classic window treatment leaves the upper sash unadorned, guests can maintain privacy while enjoying the beauty of both the traditional windows and the view outside.

Once the bed was centered below it, a small window sitting atop the wainscoting that frames this room assumed importance as a second headboard. The white window frame emphasizes that role gracefully. The window wears a Roman shade in the same floral fabric used for the pillows and comforter. The fanning pleats at the shade's lower edge echo the curves of the iron bed frame.

A woman who loves to decorate with textiles created this
pretty retreat for her daughter, layering old and new around
the room on the bed, chairs, trunk, and floor. Delicate
white batiste curtains mounted well below the window top
spill demurely to the floor; they're embellished with a small
ruffled header above the curtain rod and trimmed with
red ball fringe. That little touch of red harmonizes with the
many other rosy accents in the room.

Give three cheers for the red, white, and blue—they're as fine a decorating theme as you could want for a country daybed. This one overflows with a mix of vintage and new textiles, and is accented with some folk art pieces on the wall. Painted white to match the wall, the window itself nearly disappears, and the starry stripes clipped to a wire rod couldn't be improved as a curtain choice.

There's nothing like embroidered voile at the window to give a city bedroom a touch of country romance. With so many bright colors setting the pace here, the white looks fresh, tidy, and sweet.

With high sides, headboard, and footboard, this late-1800s Danish pine bed almost feels like an alcove retreat. The curtain spilling from the window behind it enhances that feeling of coziness. Usually a curtain hung inside the window is hemmed at the windowsill—but in this case, with extra length it becomes a soft backdrop that unifies the window and bed. Red ball fringe gives importance to the tieback and picks up the red accents in the carpet and the pillow tossed on the bed.

With bold colors and strong shapes, here's a room that successfully bridges classic country style and graphic modern décor. The cornflower blue alcove with white trim is a great setting, and its white Roman shades with deeper blue borders give the background a crisp, pleasingly linear finish that contrasts with the stylized cannonball bed.

A CLOSER LOOK

A West Virginia mountain locale inspired the décor of this bedroom, where twigs, hues of brick and moss, and a variety of textures mingle. Soothing earth tones, carved birds perched on the headboard, and a twisted driftwood-style sculpture enhance the room's rustic elegance.

1 Although the transom is left uncovered, a combination of curtains and shades on the French doors ensures a dark room at night.

2 The simple paisley curtains hang from a tree branch commandeered for service as a curtain rod.

3 The roll-up shades were made from a table runner that was in turn made from a grain sack.

4 The roll-up shades are mounted on the French doors; installed this way, the shades travel with the in-swinging doors so as not to obstruct their movement.

Various shades of ivory and white catch shadows in this sunny room, where the curtains hang high in the rafters, giving an illusion of extra height to the casement windows, and puddle luxuriously on the floor. The curtain fabric sports yellow roses set in a trellis-like tendril pattern—a nice complement to the carved foliage twining up the bedposts.

Photography Credits

Page 1: Keith Scott Morton; **Page 2** (clockwise from top left): Ellen McDermott; Keith Scott Morton; Keith Scott Morton; Steven Randazzo; **Page 3:** Ellen McDermott; **Pages 4–5:** Robin Stubbert; **Pages 6–7:** Keith Scott Morton; **Pages 8–9:** Keith Scott Morton; **Page 10:** Don Freeman; **Page 12:** Michael Weschler; **Page 13:** Keller + Keller; **Page 14:** Michael Luppino; **Page 15:** Keith Scott Morton; **Page 16:** Keith Scott Morton; **Page 17:** Steven Randazzo; **Page 18:** Keith Scott Morton; **Page 19:** Karyn Millet; **Page 20:** Keith Scott Morton; **Page 22:** Sang An; **Page 23:** Michael Skott; **Page 24:** Gridley & Graves; **Page 25:** Michael Luppino; **Page 26:** Keith Scott Morton; **Page 27:** Keith Scott Morton; **Page 28:** Keith Scott Morton; **Page 29:** David Prince; **Page 31:** John Gruen (top); Keith Scott Morton (bottom); **Page 32:** Keith Scott Morton; **Page 33:** Keith Scott Morton; **Page 34:** Keith Scott Morton; **Page 35:** Michael Luppino (left); Steven Randazzo (right); **Page 36:** Keith Scott Morton; **Page 38:** Gridley & Graves; **Page 39:** Gridley & Graves; **Page 40:** Sang An; **Page 41:** Christopher Drake; **Page 42:** Keller + Keller (top); Keith Scott Morton (bottom); **Page 43:** Laura Moss; **Page 44:** Keith Scott Morton (top); Michael Luppino (bottom); **Page 45** (clockwise from top left): Charles Schiller; Keith Scott Morton; Amber Clark; **Page 46:** Keith Scott Morton; **Page 48:** Laura Moss; **Page 49:** Jonny Valiant; **Page 50:** Gridley & Graves; **Page 51:** Stacey Brandford; **Page 52:** Michael Luppino; **Page 53:** James Merrell; **Pages 54–55:** Rob Melnychuk; **Page 56:** Keith Scott Morton; **Page 57:** Keith Scott Morton (left); Keith Scott Morton (right); **Page 58:** Ellen McDermott; **Page 59:** Keith Scott Morton; **Page 60:** Keith Scott Morton; **Page 61:** Peter Margonelli; **Page 62:** Gridley & Graves; **Page 63:** Keith Scott Morton; **Page 64:** Laura Moss; **Page 65:** Keith Scott Morton; **Page 66:** Keith Scott Morton; **Page 67:** Keith Scott Morton; **Page 68:** Robin Stubbert; **Page 69:** Keith Scott Morton; **Page 70:** Gridley & Graves; **Page 71:** Gridley & Graves (left); Keith Scott Morton (right); **Page 72:** Keith Scott Morton; **Page 73:** Keith Scott Morton; **Page 74:** Keith Scott Morton; **Page 75:** Gridley & Graves; **Page 76:** Keith Scott Morton; **Page 77:** Don Freeman; **Page 78:** Gridley & Graves; **Page 79:** Keith Scott Morton; **Page 80:** Jonn Coolidge; **Page 81:** Keith Scott Morton; **Page 82:** Jonn Coolidge; **Page 83:** Ellen McDermott; **Page 84:** Gridley & Graves; **Page 85:** Keith Scott Morton; **Page 86:** Ellen McDermott; **Page 87:** Robin Stubbert; **Page 88:** Gridley & Graves; **Page 89:** Stacey Brandford; **Page 90:** Michael Luppino; **Page 91:** Karyn Millet; **Page 92:** Steven Randazzo; **Page 93:** Jonn Coolidge; **Page 94:** Keith Scott Morton (left); Michael Weschler (right); **Page 95:** Jonny Valiant; **Page 96:** Gridley & Graves; **Page 97:** Karyn Millet; **Page 98:** Charles Maraia; **Page 99:** Gridley & Graves; **Page 100:** Laura Moss; **Page 101:** William Waldron; **Page 102:** Ellen McDermott; **Page 103:** Keith Scott Morton; **Page 104:** Jonn Coolidge; **Page 105:** Keith Scott Morton; **Page 106:** Keith Scott Morton; **Page 107:** Keith Scott Morton; **Page 108:** Keith Scott Morton; **Page 109:** Jonn Coolidge; **Page 110:** Brooke Slezak; **Page 111:** Laura Moss; **Page 112:** Keith Scott Morton; **Page 113:** Steven Randazzo (left); Miki Duisterhof (right); **Page 114:** Gridley & Graves; **Page 115:** Karyn Millet; **Page 116:** Paul Whicheloe; **Page 117:** William Waldron; **Page 118:** Thayer Allyson Gowdy; **Page 119:** Keith Scott Morton; **Page 120:** Don Freeman; **Page 121** (clockwise from top left): Joseph De Leo; Steven Randazzo; Justin Bernhaut; **Page 122:** Jonny Valiant; **Page 123:** Keith Scott Morton; **Page 124:** Keith Scott Morton; **Page 125:** Miki Duisterhof; **Page 126:** Keith Scott Morton; **Page 127:** Thayer Allyson Gowdy; **Page 128:** Robin Stubbert; **Page 129:** Michael Luppino; **Page 130:** Michael Weschler; **Page 131:** Jonn Coolidge; **Page 132:** Don Freeman; **Page 134:** Jonn Coolidge; **Page 135:** Helen Norman; **Page 136:** Laura Moss; **Page 137:** David Prince; **Page 138:** Michael Weschler; **Page 139:** Keller + Keller; **Page 140:** Gridley & Graves; **Page 141:** Keith Scott Morton (left); Steven Randazzo (right); **Page 142:** Keith Scott Morton; **Page 143:** Keith Scott Morton; **Page 144:** Laura Moss; **Page 145:** Keith Scott Morton; **Page 146:** Michael Partenio; **Page 147:** Gridley & Graves; **Page 148:** Gridley & Graves; **Page 149:** Keith Scott Morton; **Page 150:** Keller + Keller; **Page 151:** Keith Scott Morton; **Page 152:** Keith Scott Morton; **Page 153:** Keith Scott Morton

Front Cover (clockwise from top right): Paul Whicheloe, Keith Scott Morton, Laura Moss, Keith Scott Morton

Back Cover (clockwise from top right): Laura Moss, Sang An, Jonn Coolidge, William P. Steele

Index